ENGLISH TOWN

FOR EVERYONE

STARTER

BOOK

3

Contents

Characters

Hello Song

Hello, everyone.
Hello, teacher!
Hello, friends!

Let's have fun together.
We'll have a good time.

Are you ready to start?
We're ready!

Here we go!

Goodbye Song

Did you have fun?

It's time to say goodbye.
See you next time!
See you next time!

Did you enjoy the class?
Yes! We had a fun time!
Yes! We had a fun time!

See you later! See you later!
Goodbye. Goodbye.

Bye! Bye!

At Home

 **Talk**

Look, listen, and repeat.

Hi. Please come in.

Thanks.

Mom, this is Ben.
Ben, this is my mom.

Nice to meet you, Ben.

Say and Act

Hi. Please come in.

Thanks.

Learn

A. Listen and repeat. Make sentences.

1	2	3	4
mom	dad	grandma	grandpa

A: This is my _____.
B: Nice to meet you.

B. Listen, point, and say.

C. Listen and sing.

Please Come In

Hi. Hi. Hi.
Please come in.
Thanks. Thanks.
Mom, mom.
This is my mom.
Nice to meet you.

Hi. Hi. Hi.
Please come in.
Thanks. Thanks.
Dad, dad.
This is my dad.
Nice to meet you.

Activity

A. Listen and number.

teacher

e-learning

B. Say and answer.

A: This is my _____.
B: Nice to meet you.

1

mom

2

dad

3

friend

4

teacher

5

grandma

6

grandpa

C. Draw, say, and write.

A: This is my dad.
B: Nice to meet you.

This is my dad.

This is my _____.

Family

 **Talk**

Look, listen, and repeat.

Have a seat.

Thank you.

Who is she?

She's my sister.

Have a seat.

Thank you.

 **Learn**

A. Listen and repeat. Make sentences.

He/She's my _____.

1	2	3	4
uncle	aunt	brother	sister

B. Listen, point, and say.

A: Who is he/she?
B: He/She's my _____.

C. Listen and sing.

Who Is She?

Have a seat. Have a seat.
Thank you. Thank you.

Who, who? Who is she?
Sister, sister.
She's my sister.

Have a seat. Have a seat.
Thank you. Thank you.

Who, who? Who is he?
Brother, brother.
He's my brother.

Activity

A. Listen and circle.

1

2

3

4

B. Ask and answer.

A: Who is he/she?
B: He/She's my _____.

1
mom

2
dad

3
sister

4
brother

5
aunt

6
uncle

C. Draw, ask, and answer.

A: Who is she?
B: She's my mom.

A: Who is he?
B: He's my dad.

Example

grandpa grandma   grandpa grandma

uncle   mom   dad   aunt

me

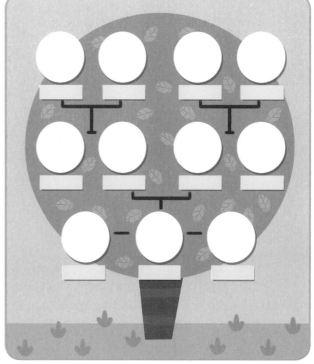

This Is My Mom

Bobo   Penny

A. Listen and repeat.

B. Listen and number.

C. Read and match.

1. She is _____. •   • Bobo's brother

2. He is _____. •   • Penny

3. This is _____. •   • Bobo's mom

D. Speak with your partner.

1

2

 **Play**

A. Listen and chant.

This Is My Uncle

Please come in. Have a seat.
Thanks.
Who, who? Who is he?
Uncle, uncle. He's my uncle.
This is my uncle.

Please come in. Have a seat.
Thanks.
Who, who? Who is she?
Aunt, aunt. She's my aunt.
This is my aunt.

B. Play a game.

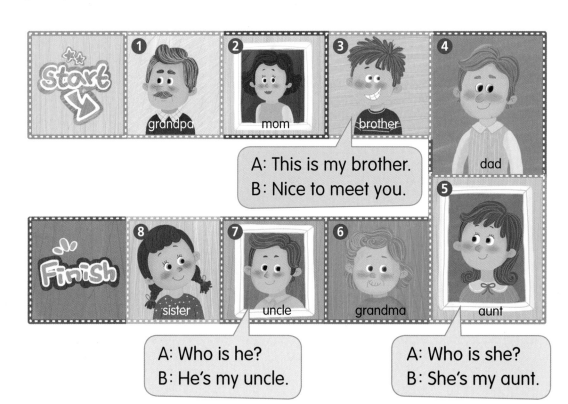

Start

❶ grandpa
❷ mom
❸ brother
❹ dad
❺ aunt
❻ grandma
❼ uncle
❽ sister

Finish

A: This is my brother.
B: Nice to meet you.

A: Who is he?
B: He's my uncle.

A: Who is she?
B: She's my aunt.

Reading Time

I Love My Family

She is my mom.
She works too much.

He is my dad.
He always plays with us.

He is my brother.
He always smiles.

This is me. I like singing.
I love my family.

Read and circle.

1. _____ works too much.   **a** My mom   **b** My dad
2. _____ always smiles.   **a** My dad   **b** My brother

Rooms

 Talk

Look, listen, and repeat.

Come with me.

Okay.

This is the kitchen.

Wow, it's nice.

Come with me.

Okay.

Learn

A. Listen and repeat. Make sentences.

This is the _____.

bathroom   bedroom   kitchen   living room

B. Listen, point, and say.

A: This is the _____.
B: Wow, it's nice.

C. Listen and sing.

Come with Me

Come with me.
Okay. Okay.
This is the living room.
Wow, it's nice.

Come with me.
Okay. Okay.
This is the kitchen.
Wow, it's nice.

 Activity

A. Listen and choose O or X.

1

O
X

2

O
X

3

O
X

4
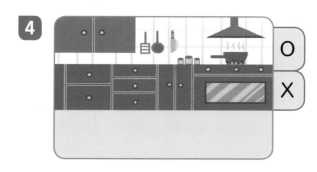
O
X

B. Say and answer.

A: This is the _____.
B: Wow, it's nice.

1

living room

2

bathroom

3

kitchen

4

bedroom

5

art room

6

music room

C. Draw, point, and say.

A: This is the bathroom.
B: Wow, it's nice.

Example

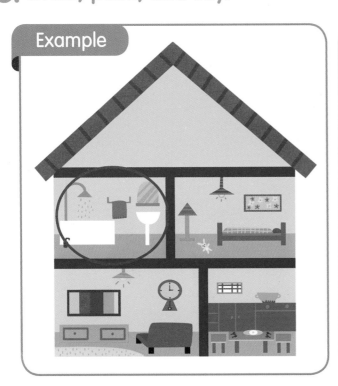

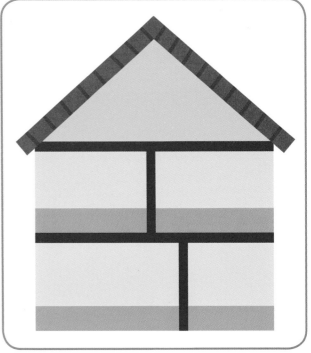

Furniture

 **Talk**

Look, listen, and repeat.

May I use your bathroom?

Sure.

Learn

A. Listen and repeat. Make sentences.

There is my _____.

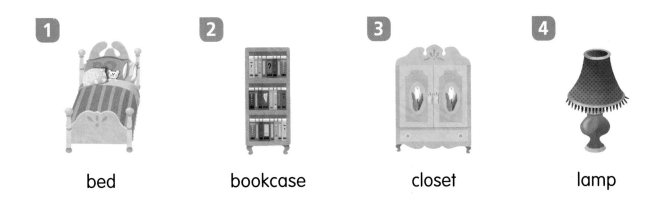

1	2	3	4
bed	bookcase	closet	lamp

B. Listen, point, and say.

A: There is my _____.
B: It looks nice.

C. Listen and sing.

There Is My Bed

May I use your bathroom?
Sure, sure!

This is my room.
There is my bed.
It looks nice!

May I use your bathroom?
Sure, sure!

This is my room.
There is my lamp.
It looks nice!

 Activity

A. Look and match.

1 There is my closet. •

2 There is my lamp. •

3 There is my bookcase. •

24

e-learning

B. Say and answer.

A: There is my _____.
B: It looks nice.

1 desk

2 bed

3 lamp

4 closet

5 bookcase

6 computer

C. Connect, color, and say.

A: There is my bed.
B: It looks nice.

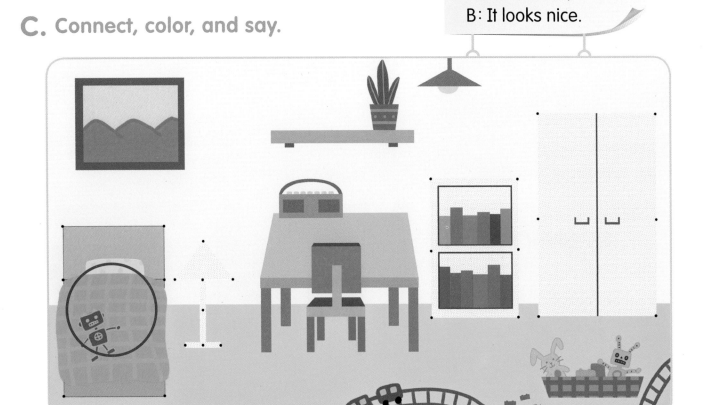

This Is the Kitchen

Polly

A. Listen and repeat.

B. Listen and circle.

1

a b

2

a b

3

a b

C. Read and choose T or F.

1 Polly's bed looks nice.　　T　F

2 Bobo can use Polly's bedroom.　　T　F

D. Speak with your partner.

1

Wow, it's nice.

2

It looks nice.

 **Play**

This Is My Room

Come, come. Come with me.
This is the bedroom.
Wow, it's nice. Wow, it's nice.
Room, room. This is my room.
There is my bed. There is my bed.
It looks nice. It looks nice.

Come, come. Come with me.
This is the bathroom.
Wow, it's nice. Wow, it's nice.
Room, room. This is my room.
There is my closet. There is my closet.
It looks nice. It looks nice.

B. Play a game.

A: There is my bed.
B: It looks nice.

A: This is the bathroom.
B: Wow, it's nice.

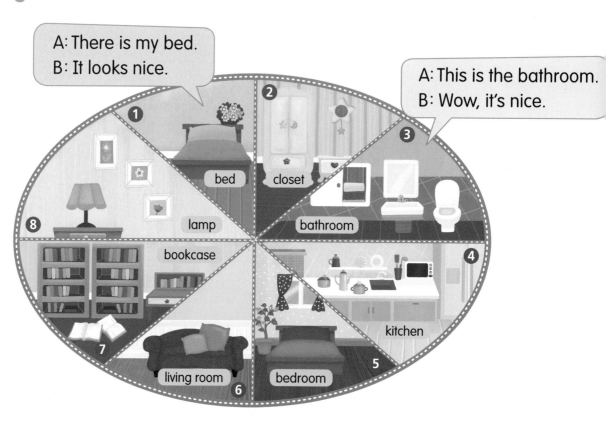

Reading Time

e-learning

This is our tree house.
My brother and I play here.

The tree house is small.
There is only one room.

There is a bed.
There is a treasure box.

We like our tree house.
Come and play with us.

Read and circle.

1. What is in the tree house?   **a** A bed   **b** A bookcase
2. Who plays in the tree house with me?   **a** My sister   **b** My brother

Lesson 7 Possessions

 Talk

Look, listen, and repeat.

Do you like puppies?

Sure. I love them.

Do you have horses?

Yes, I do.

 Say and Act

Do you like puppies?

Sure. I love them.

30

Learn

A. Listen and repeat. Make sentences.

Do you have _____?

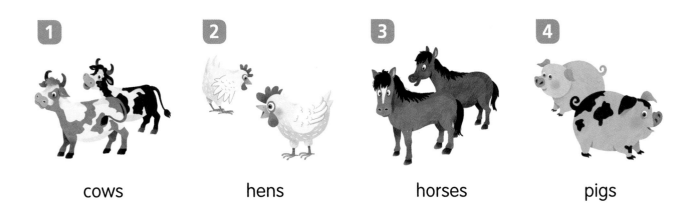

1 cows

2 hens

3 horses

4 pigs

B. Listen, point, and say.

A: Do you have _____?
B: Yes, I do.

C. Listen and sing.

Do You Have Hens?

Do you have hens?
Yes, yes. Yes, I do.
Do you like hens?
Sure, sure. I love them.

Do you have horses?
Yes, yes. Yes, I do.
Do you like horses?
Sure, sure. I love them.

 Activity

A. Listen and number.

B. Ask and answer.

A: Do you have _____?
B: Yes, I do.

1 horses

2 puppies

3 cows

4 pigs

5 hens

6 rabbits

C. Check, ask, and answer.

A: Do you have horses?
B: Yes, I do.

	horses	puppies	cows	pigs	hens	rabbits
I	✔					
My Friend						

Lesson 8

 **Talk**

Look, listen, and repeat.

Sure, you can.

Can I touch them?

How many eggs do you have?

I have 11 eggs.

 Say and Act

Can I touch them?

Sure, you can.

 **Learn**

A. Listen and repeat. Make sentences.

I have _____ eggs.

1 **11**
eleven

2 **12**
twelve

3 **13**
thirteen

4 **14**
fourteen

5 **15**
fifteen

A: How many _____ do you have?
B: I have _____ _____.

B. Listen, point, and say.

3 apples

4 lemons

2 pencils

1 pencil cases

5 doughnuts

C. Listen and sing.

How Many Eggs Do You Have?

Eggs, eggs.
How many eggs do you have?
Eleven, eleven. I have eleven.
Can I touch them?
Sure. Sure, you can.

Cookies, cookies.
How many cookies do you have?
Twelve, twelve. I have twelve.
Can I touch them?
Sure. Sure, you can.

Activity

A. Listen and circle.

36

B. Ask and answer.

A: How many eggs do you have?
B: I have _____ eggs.

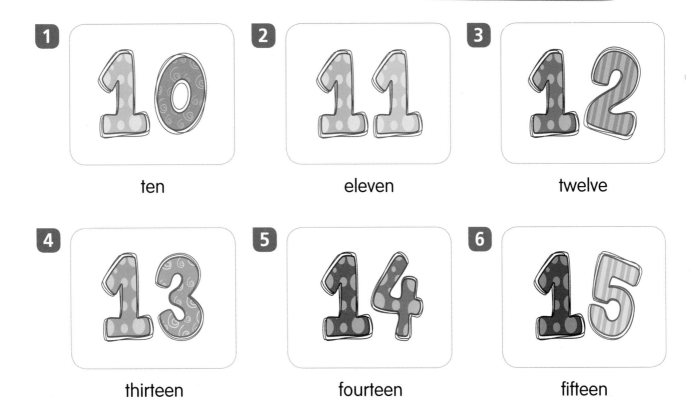

1 ten

2 eleven

3 twelve

4 thirteen

5 fourteen

6 fifteen

C. Find, color, and say.

A: How many _____ do you have?
B: I have _____ _____.

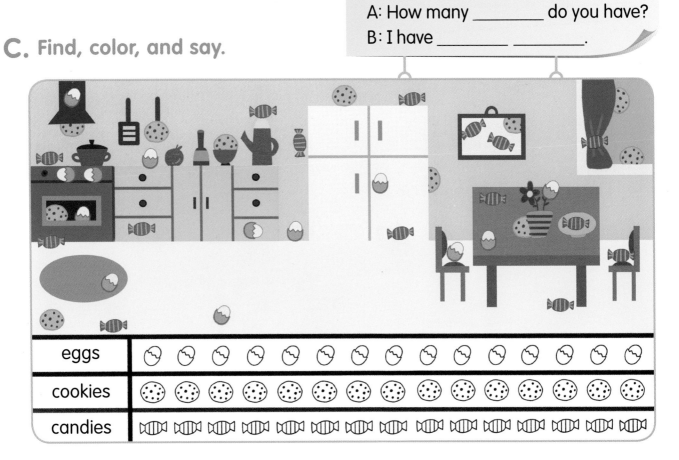

eggs		
cookies		
candies		

Do You Have Eggs?

Henny

A. Listen and repeat.

B. Listen and choose O or X.

1

O   X

2

O   X

3

O   X

C. Read and circle.

1 Wawa _____ chickens.   ⓐ likes   ⓑ has

2 Henny has _____ eggs.   ⓐ thirteen   ⓑ fifteen

D. Speak with your partner.

 **Play**

A. Listen and chant.

Do You Have Pigs?

Pigs, pigs. Do you have pigs?
Yes, yes. Yes, I do. I have pigs.
How many pigs do you have?
Eleven, eleven. I have eleven.

Cows, cows. Do you have cows?
Yes, yes. Yes, I do. I have cows.
How many cows do you have?
Twelve, twelve. I have twelve.

B. Play a game.

A: Do you like horses?
B: Sure. I love them.

A: How many eggs do you have?
B: I have twelve eggs.

Reading Time

e-learning

Where Are the Eggs?

Can you see the eggs?
There are 11 eggs in the nest.

A hen sits on the eggs all day long.
She sits on them for 22 days.

Oh, the hen is not in her nest.
There are no eggs.

Wow, there are little yellow chicks.
The eggs became chicks.

Read and circle.

1. There are _____ eggs in the nest.   **a** eleven   **b** thirteen

2. A hen sits on the eggs for _____ days.   **a** twenty-two   **b** twenty-four

Assessment Test 1

🎧 **Listening**

A. Listen and check.

1 ☐ ☐ ☐ ☐

2 ☐ ☐ ☐ ☐

3 11 ☐   12 ☐   13 ☐   14 ☐

B. Listen and choose O or X.

1 O X   2 O X   3 O X

4 O X   5 O X   6 O X

C. Listen and circle.

D. Listen and number.

Reading Read and number.

1. I like horses.
2. Have a seat.
3. This is my dad.
4. There is my closet.
5. This is the living room.
6. I have thirteen eggs.

 Writing Match and trace.

1    •   •   This is my brother.

2    •   •   She's my sister.

3    •   •   I have fourteen cows.

4    •   •   There is my lamp.

44

 # Speaking

A. Listen, point, and answer.

B. Listen and answer.

1
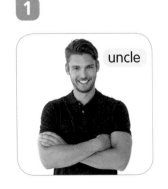
uncle

2

3

4

Lesson 11 Foods

 Talk

Look, listen, and repeat.

 Say and Act

It smells good.

Yes, it does!

Learn

A. Listen and repeat. Make sentences.

1 noodles

2 salad

3 soup

4 steak

B. Listen, point, and say.

A: Would you like some _____?
B: Yes, please.

C. Listen and sing.

Would You Like Some Salad?

It smells good. It smells good.
Yes, yes. Yes, it does.
Would you like some salad?
Yes, please. Yes, please.

It smells good. It smells good.
Yes, yes. Yes, it does.
Would you like some noodles?
Yes, please. Yes, please.

 Activity

A. Look and match.

Yes, please.

1 Would you like some noodles? •

2 Would you like some steak? •

3 Would you like some salad? •

B. Ask and answer.

1

soup

2

noodles

3

bread

4

steak

5

fish

6

salad

C. Check, ask, and answer.

A: Would you like some soup?
B: Yes, please.

	soup	noodles	bread	steak	fish	salad
I	✔					
My Friend						

Lesson 12 Desserts

 **Talk**

Look, listen, and repeat.

 Say and Act

Help yourself.

Thank you.

Learn

A. Listen and repeat. Make sentences.

I want some _____.

1

crackers

2

ice cream

3

pie

4

pudding

A: What do you want for dessert?
B: I want some _____.

B. Listen, point, and say.

C. Listen and sing.

Help Yourself

What do you want for dessert?
I want some pudding.
Help yourself. Help yourself.
Oh, thank you.

What do you want for dessert?
I want some pie.
Help yourself. Help yourself.
Oh, thank you.

Activity

A. Listen and choose T or F.

1
T
F

2
T
F

3
T
F

4
T
F

B. Ask and answer.

A: What do you want for dessert?
B: I want some _____.

1

pudding

2
crackers

3

yogurt

4

pie

5

ice cream

6

doughnuts

A: What do you want for dessert?
B: I want some ice cream.

C. Color, ask, and answer.

My Desserts

My Friend's Desserts

It Smells Good

A. Listen and repeat.

B. Listen and number.

C. Read and circle.

I want some doughnuts, ice cream, and cookies.

D. Speak with your partner.

1
Yes, it does!

2
Yes, please.

 **Play**

A. Listen and chant.

It Smells Good

It smells good. It smells good.
Would you like some soup?
Yes, please. Yes, please. I like soup.
Help yourself. Help yourself.

It smells good. It smells good.
What do you want for dessert?
Pudding, pudding. I want some pudding.
Help yourself. Help yourself.

B. Play a game.

A: What do you want for dessert?
B: I want some pudding.

A: Would you like some salad?
B: Yes, please.

Reading Time

Banana Smoothie

What do you want for dessert?
Would you like a banana smoothie?

Peel, cut, and put the banana
in the refrigerator. Let it freeze.

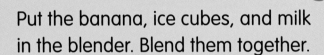

Put the banana, ice cubes, and milk
in the blender. Blend them together.

Your banana smoothie is ready.
Help yourself!

Read and circle.

1. What is for dessert?

     a banana pudding

     b banana smoothie

2. What is <u>not</u> needed for the dessert?

     a yogurt   **b** milk

Outdoor Fun

 Talk

Look, listen, and repeat.

 Say and Act

Let's go outside.

That's a good idea.

Learn

A. Listen and repeat. Make sentences.

What a nice _____!

1 **2** **3** **4**

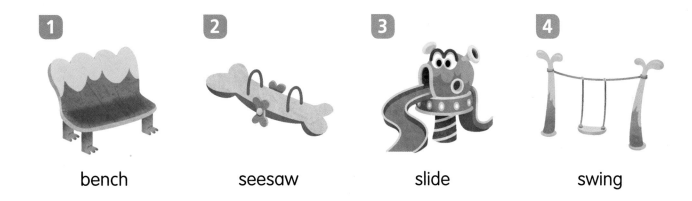

bench   seesaw   slide   swing

B. Listen, point, and say.

A: What a nice _____!
B: I think so, too.

C. Listen and sing.

Let's Go Outside

Let's go outside.
That's a good idea.
Slide. What a nice slide!
I think so, too.

Let's go outside.
That's a good idea.
Swing. What a nice swing!
I think so, too.

 Activity

A. Listen and number.

B. Say and answer.

A: What a nice _____!
B: I think so, too.

1 swing

2 seesaw

3 jump rope

4 bench

5 slide

6 yo-yo

C. Connect, color, and say.

A: What a nice slide!
B: I think so, too.

Lesson 15

Describing Things

 **Talk**

Look, listen, and repeat.

Can you help me?

Okay. I'm coming.

What does it look like?

It's big.

 Say and Act

Can you help me?

Okay. I'm coming.

Learn

A. Listen and repeat. Make sentences.

It's _____.

1	2	3	4
big	small	long	short

B. Listen, point, and say.

A: What does it look like?
B: It's _____.

What Does It Look Like?

Can you help me?
Okay. I'm coming.

What does it look like?
It's big and yellow.

Can you help me?
Okay. I'm coming.

What does it look like?
It's small and red.

Activity

A. Look, match, and trace.

 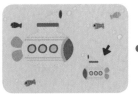 • • It's small and yellow.

  • • It's square and orange.

 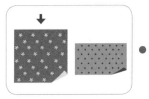 • • It's long and yellow.

64

B. Ask and answer.

A: What does it look like?
B: It's _____.

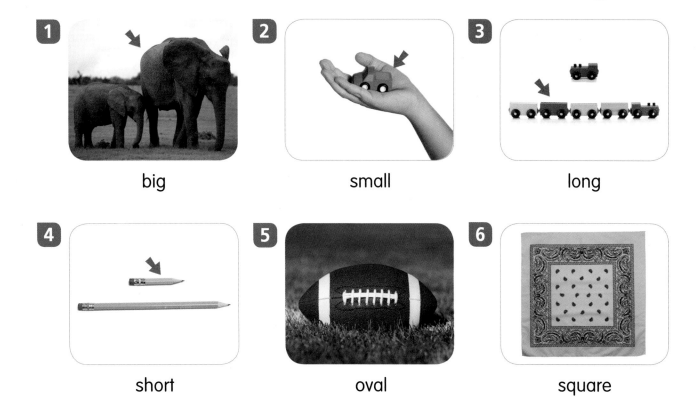

1 big

2 small

3 long

4 short

5 oval

6 square

A: What does it look like?
B: It's big.

C. Ask, answer, and write.

long　　short　　small

It's big.

It's ____.

It's ____.

It's ____.

What a Nice Slide!

A. Listen and repeat.

B. Listen and circle.

1

a b

2

a b

3

a b

C. Read and choose T or F.

1 Polly's slide is nice.　　　T　　F

2 Wawa's ball is big and red.　　T　　F

D. Speak with your partner.

1

I think so, too.

2 What does it look like?

 **Play**

A. Listen and chant.

What a Nice Seesaw!

Outside, outside. Let's go outside.

That's a good idea. That's a good idea.

What a nice seesaw! (Wow!)

What does it look like?

It's big and yellow.

Outside, outside. Let's go outside.

That's a good idea. That's a good idea.

What a nice bench! (Wow!)

What does it look like?

It's long and blue.

B. Play a game.

A: What a nice seesaw!
B: I think so, too.

A: What does it look like?
B: It's long.

Reading Time

e-learning

This is the Statue of Liberty in the U.S.
It's very big and tall.

This is the Eiffel Tower in France.
It's very tall.

This is the Great Wall of China.
It's very long.

This is Big Ben in England.
It's very big and beautiful.
What a big clock!

Read and circle.

1. The Great Wall is in _____.   **a** France   **b** China
2. The Statue of Liberty is big and _____.   **a** short   **b** tall

Lesson 17 Things to Read

 **Talk**

Look, listen, and repeat.

I had fun.

Me, too.

What are you doing?

I'm reading a book.

 Say and Act

I had fun.

Me, too.

Learn

A. Listen and repeat. Make sentences.

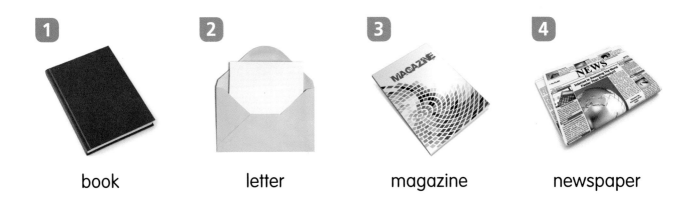

1	2	3	4
book	letter	magazine	newspaper

B. Listen, point, and say.

A: What are you doing?
B: I'm reading a _____.

C. Listen and sing.

What Are You Doing?

What, what? What are you doing?
Book, book.
I'm reading a book.

Oh, I had fun. Oh, I had fun.
Oh, oh, oh. Me, too.

What, what? What are you doing?
Newspaper, newspaper.
I'm reading a newspaper.

Oh, I had fun. Oh, I had fun.
Oh, oh, oh. Me, too.

Activity

A. Listen and circle.

B. Ask and answer.

A: What are you doing?
B: I'm reading _____.

1

a newspaper

2

a book

3

a letter

4

a magazine

5

an e-mail

6

a postcard

C. Check, ask, and answer.

A: What are you doing?
B: I'm reading a book.

	book	letter	magazine	newspaper
I	✓			
My Friend				

Fruit Trees

 Talk

Look, listen, and repeat.

Can I come again?

Of course.

What is he doing?

He's planting a lemon tree.

Can I come again?

Of course.

74

Learn

A. Listen and repeat. Make sentences.

He's planting a _____ tree.

1

lemon

2

mango

3

peach

4

pear

B. Listen, point, and say.

A: What is he doing?
B: He's planting a _____ tree.

C. Listen and sing.

What Is He Doing?

Can I come again?
Of course! Of course!

What is he doing?
He's planting a lemon tree.

Can I come again?
Of course! Of course!

What is he doing?
He's planting a mango tree.

Activity

A. Listen and choose T or F.

1 T F

2 T F

3 T F

4 T F

B. Ask and answer.

A: What is he doing?
B: He's planting _____.

1 a peach tree

2 a lemon tree

3 an orange tree

4 an apple tree

5 a mango tree

6 a pear tree

C. Draw, ask, and answer.

A: What is he doing?
B: He's planting a mango tree.

Example

What Are You Doing?

A. Listen and repeat.

B. Listen and choose O or X.

1

O X

2

O X

3

O X

C. Read and match.

1 Bobo came to _____.   •   • a mango tree

2 Penny is reading _____.   •   • a magazine

3 The monkey is planting _____. •   • Penny's house

D. Speak with your partner.

1

2

 **Play**

A. Listen and chant.

What Are You Doing?

What, what? What are you doing?
(clap, clap) I'm reading a letter.

What, what? What is he doing?
(clap, clap) He's planting a peach tree.

Can I come again?
Of course. Yeah!

What, what? What are you doing?
(clap, clap) I'm reading a magazine.

What, what? What is he doing?
(clap, clap) He's planting a pear tree.

Can I come again?
Of course. Yeah!

B. Play a game.

A: What are you doing?
B: I'm reading a newspaper.

A: What is he doing?
B: He's planting a mango tree.

Reading Time

I Love Apples

This is my dad.
He is planting an apple tree.

There are many apples on the tree.
Let's pick and eat them.

How shall we eat them?
An apple pie? Apple juice? Apple jam?
Oh, I love them all.

But the best is to eat them fresh.
Yummy!

Read and circle.

1. The girl's dad is planting _____. **a** a peach tree **b** an apple tree

2. The girl is going to eat _____. **a** fresh apples

   b some apple ice cream

Assessment Test 2

 Listening

A. Listen and check.

1

☐   ☐   ☐   ☐

2

☐   ☐   ☐   ☐

3

☐   ☐   ☐   ☐

B. Listen and choose O or X.

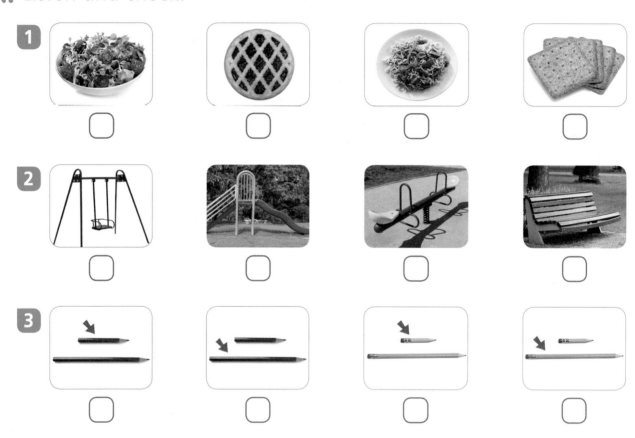

C. Listen and circle.

D. Listen and number.

Reading Read and check.

1. It's small and yellow.

2. Would you like some noodles?

3. I'm reading a book.

4. I want some crackers.

5. What a nice slide!

6. He's planting a peach tree.

 Writing Match and trace.

1  · · It's small.

2  · · I want some pie.

3  · · I'm reading a book.

4  · · What a nice seesaw!

 **Speaking**

A. Listen, point, and answer.

B. Listen and answer.

Syllabus

Lesson	Topic	Language	Key Vocabulary
Lesson 1	At Home	Mom, this is Ben. Ben, this is my mom. - Nice to meet you, Ben. Hi. Please come in. - Thanks.	mom dad grandma grandpa
Lesson 2	Family	Who is she? - She's my sister. Have a seat. - Thank you.	uncle aunt brother sister
Lesson 3	Step Up 1	Story: This Is My Mom Lessons 1~2 Review * Reading Time: I Love My Family	
Lesson 4	Rooms	This is the kitchen. - Wow, it's nice. Come with me. - Okay.	bathroom bedroom kitchen living room
Lesson 5	Furniture	There is my bed. - It looks nice. May I use your bathroom? - Sure.	bed bookcase closet lamp
Lesson 6	Step Up 2	Story: This Is the Kitchen Lessons 4~5 Review * Reading Time: Our Tree House	
Lesson 7	Possessions	Do you have horses? - Yes, I do. Do you like puppies? - Sure. I love them.	cows hens horses pigs
Lesson 8	Numbers	How many eggs do you have? - I have 11 eggs. Can I touch them? - Sure, you can.	eleven twelve thirteen fourteen fifteen
Lesson 9	Step Up 3	Story: Do You Have Eggs? Lessons 7~8 Review * Reading Time: Where Are the Eggs?	
Lesson 10		**Assessment Test 1** Lessons 1~9 Review	

Lesson	Topic	Language	Key Vocabulary
Lesson 11	Foods	Would you like some noodles? - Yes, please. It smells good. - Yes, it does!	noodles salad soup steak
Lesson 12	Desserts	What do you want for dessert? - I want some pudding. Help yourself. - Thank you.	crackers ice cream pie pudding
Lesson 13	Step Up 4	Story: It Smells Good Lessons 11~12 Review * Reading Time: Banana Smoothie	
Lesson 14	Outdoor Fun	What a nice slide! - I think so, too. Let's go outside. - That's a good idea.	bench seesaw slide swing
Lesson 15	Describing Things	What does it look like? - It's big. Can you help me? - Okay. I'm coming.	big small long short
Lesson 16	Step Up 5	Story: What a Nice Slide! Lessons 14~15 Review * Reading Time: What a Big Clock!	
Lesson 17	Things to Read	What are you doing? - I'm reading a book. I had fun. - Me, too.	book letter magazine newspaper
Lesson 18	Fruit Trees	What is he doing? - He's planting a lemon tree. Can I come again? - Of course.	lemon mango peach pear
Lesson 19	Step Up 6	Story: What Are You Doing? Lessons 17~18 Review * Reading Time: I Love Apples	
Lesson 20	Assessment Test 2 Lessons 11~19 Review		

Flashcard List

mom	dad	grandma
grandpa	uncle	aunt
brother	sister	bathroom
bedroom	kitchen	living room
bed	bookcase	closet
lamp	cows	hens
horses	pigs	eleven
twelve	thirteen	fourteen
fifteen	noodles	salad
soup	steak	crackers
ice cream	pie	pudding
bench	seesaw	swing
slide	big	small
long	short	book
letter	magazine	newspaper
lemon	mango	peach
pear		

Lesson 1 At Home

	Vocabulary	Meaning	Sentence
1	come	오다, 가다	Please come in.
2	dad	아빠	This is my dad.
3	grandma	할머니	This is my grandma.
4	grandpa	할아버지	This is my grandpa.
5	in	~에	Please come in.
6	meet	만나다	Nice to meet you.
7	mom	엄마	This is my mom.
8	nice	좋은	Nice to meet you.
9	please	제발	Please come in.
10	this	이 사람, 이것	This is Ben.

Lesson 2 Family

	Vocabulary	Meaning	Sentence
1	aunt	고모, 이모, 숙모	She's my aunt.
2	brother	남자 형제	He's my brother.
3	have	가지다	Have a seat.
4	he	그, 그 분	Who is he?
5	my	나의, 내	He's my brother.
6	seat	자리, 좌석	Have a seat.
7	she	그녀	Who is she?
8	sister	여자 형제	She's my sister.
9	uncle	삼촌, 외삼촌, 고모부, 이모부	He's my uncle.
10	who	누구	Who is he?

Lesson 5 Furniture

	Vocabulary	Meaning	Sentence
1	bed	침대	This is my bed.
2	bookcase	책장	This is my bookcase.
3	closet	옷장	This is my closet.
4	computer	컴퓨터	This is my computer.
5	desk	책상	This is my desk.
6	lamp	램프, 등	This is my lamp.
7	look	~해 보이다	It looks nice.
8	may	~해도 되다	May I use your bathroom?
9	my	나의	This is my room.
10	use	쓰다, 사용하다	May I use your bathroom?

Lesson 6 This Is the Kitchen

	Vocabulary	Meaning	Sentence
1	and	~와/과	My brother and I play here.
2	here	여기에	My brother and I play here.
3	kitchen	부엌	This is the kitchen.
4	only	유일한	There is only one room.
5	small	작은	The tree house is small.
6	there is	~에 있다	There is only one room.
7	treasure box	보물 상자	There is a treasure box.
8	tree house	나무 위의 집	This is our tree house.
9	us	우리	Come and play with us.
10	with	~와 함께	Come and play with us.

Lesson 3 This Is My Mom

	Vocabulary	Meaning	Sentence
1	always	항상, 언제나	He always smiles.
2	brother	남자 형제	He is my brother.
3	family	가족	I love my family.
4	much	많은	She works too much.
5	play	놀다	He always plays with us.
6	please	제발	Please come in.
7	sing	노래하다	I like singing.
8	smile	미소 짓다	He always smiles.
9	who	누구	Who is he?
10	work	일하다	She works too much.

Lesson 4 Rooms

	Vocabulary	Meaning	Sentence
1	bathroom	욕실, 화장실	This is the bathroom.
2	bedroom	침실	This is the bedroom.
3	come	오다, 가다	Come with me.
4	kitchen	부엌	This is the kitchen.
5	living room	거실	This is the living room.
6	me	나, 나에게	Come with me.
7	nice	좋은	It's nice.
8	this	이것	This is the bedroom.
9	with	～와 함께	Come with me.
10	wow	와, 우와	Wow, it's nice.

Lesson 7 Possessions

	Vocabulary	Meaning	Sentence
1	cow	소	Do you have cows?
2	have	가지다	Do you have cows?
3	hen	암탉	Do you have hens?
4	horse	말	Do you have horses?
5	like	좋아하다	Do you like puppies?
6	love	사랑하다	I love them.
7	pig	돼지	Do you have pigs?
8	puppy	강아지	Do you like puppies?
9	rabbit	토끼	Do you have rabbits?
10	them	그들	I love them.

Lesson 8 Numbers

	Vocabulary	Meaning	Sentence
1	can	～할 수 있다	Can I touch them?
2	egg	달걀	How many eggs do you have?
3	how	어떻게	How many eggs do you have?
4	many	많은	How many eggs do you have?
5	touch	만지다	Can I touch them?
6	eleven	열 하나, 11	I have eleven eggs.
7	twelve	열 둘, 12	I have twelve eggs.
8	thirteen	열 셋, 13	I have thirteen eggs.
9	fourteen	열 넷, 14	I have fourteen eggs.
10	fifteen	열 다섯, 15	I have fifteen eggs.

Lesson 9 Do You Have Eggs?

	Vocabulary	Meaning	Sentence
1	become	~이 되다	The eggs became chicks.
2	chicken	닭	Do you like chickens?
3	chick	병아리	The eggs became chicks.
4	day	하루	She sits on them for 22 days.
5	egg	달걀	Can you see the eggs?
6	little	작은	There are little yellow chicks.
7	nest	둥지	There are 11 eggs in the nest.
8	sit	앉다	She sits on them for 22 days.
9	touch	만지다	Can I touch them?
10	yellow	노란색의	There are little yellow chicks.

Lesson 11 Foods

	Vocabulary	Meaning	Sentence
1	bread	빵	Would you like some bread?
2	fish	(물)고기	Would you like some fish?
3	good	좋은	It smells good.
4	noodle	국수	Would you like some noodles?
5	salad	샐러드	Would you like some salad?
6	smell	냄새가 나다	It smells good.
7	some	조금	Would you like some noodles?
8	soup	수프	Would you like some soup?
9	steak	스테이크	Would you like some steak?
10	would	~ 할 것이다	Would you like some fish?

Lesson 14 Outdoor Fun

	Vocabulary	Meaning	Sentence
1	bench	벤치	What a nice bench!
2	idea	생각	That's a good idea.
3	jump rope	줄넘기	What a nice jump rope!
4	outside	밖	Let's go outside.
5	seesaw	시소	What a nice seesaw!
6	slide	미끄럼틀	What a nice slide!
7	swing	그네	What a nice swing!
8	think	~라고 생각하다	I think so, too.
9	too	~또한	I think so, too.
10	yo-yo	요요	What a nice yo-yo!

Lesson 15 Describing Things

	Vocabulary	Meaning	Sentence
1	big	큰	It's big.
2	can	~할 수 있다	Can you help me?
3	come	오다, 가다	I'm coming.
4	help	돕다	Can you help me?
5	long	긴	It's long.
6	oval	타원형의	It's oval.
7	red	빨간색	It's small and red.
8	short	짧은	It's short.
9	small	작은	It's small.
10	square	정사각형의	It's square.

Lesson 12 Desserts

	Vocabulary	Meaning	Sentence
1	cracker	크래커	I want some crackers.
2	dessert	디저트	What do you want for dessert?
3	for	위한	What do you want for dessert?
4	help	돕다	Help yourself.
5	ice cream	아이스크림	I want some ice cream.
6	pie	파이	I want some pie.
7	pudding	푸딩	I want some pudding.
8	want	원하다	I want some crackers.
9	what	무엇	What do you want for dessert?
10	yourself	너 자신	Help yourself.

Lesson 13 It Smells Good

	Vocabulary	Meaning	Sentence
1	banana	바나나	Your banana smoothie is ready.
2	blender	믹서	Put the banana in the blender.
3	cut	자르다	Cut the banana.
4	dessert	디저트	What do you want for dessert?
5	freeze	얼다	Let it freeze.
6	peel	껍질을 벗기다	Peel the banana.
7	put	넣다	Put the banana in the blender.
8	refrigerator	냉장고	Put the banana in the refrigerator.
9	smell	냄새가 나다	It smells good.
10	smoothie	스무디	Would you like a banana smoothie?

Lesson 16 What a Nice Slide!

	Vocabulary	Meaning	Sentence
1	beautiful	아름다운	It's very big and beautiful.
2	big	큰	It's very big and tall.
3	clock	시계	What a big clock!
4	idea	생각	That's a good idea.
5	look	～처럼 보이다	What does it look like?
6	much	많은	Thank you so much.
7	nice	좋은	What a nice slide!
8	outside	밖, 바깥쪽	Let's go outside.
9	very	매우	It's very tall.
10	seesaw	시소	What a nice seesaw!

Lesson 17 Things to Read

	Vocabulary	Meaning	Sentence
1	book	책	I'm reading a book.
2	e-mail	이메일	I'm reading an e-mail.
3	fun	재미	I had fun.
4	had	have(가지다)의 과거형	I had fun.
5	letter	편지	I'm reading a letter.
6	magazine	잡지	I'm reading a magazine.
7	newspaper	신문	I'm reading a newspaper.
8	postcard	엽서	I'm reading a postcard.
9	read	읽다	I'm reading a book.
10	what	무엇	What are you doing?

Lesson 18 Fruit Trees

	Vocabulary	Meaning	Sentence
1	again	다시	Can I come again?
2	apple	사과	He's planting an apple tree.
3	course	물론	Of course.
4	lemon	레몬	He's planting a lemon tree.
5	mango	망고	He's planting a mango tree.
6	orange	오렌지	He's planting an orange tree.
7	peach	복숭아	He's planting a peach tree.
8	pear	배	He's planting a pear tree.
9	plant	심다	He's planting a lemon tree.
10	tree	나무	He's planting a mango tree.

Lesson 19 What Are You Doing?

	Vocabulary	Meaning	Sentence
1	all	모든	I love them all.
2	best	최상의	But the best is to eat them fresh.
3	eat	먹다	How shall we eat them?
4	fresh	신선한	But the best is to eat them fresh.
5	how	어떻게	How shall we eat them?
6	mango	망고	She's planting a mango tree.
7	pick	따다	Let's pick and eat them.
8	plant	심다	She's planting a mango tree.
9	there are	~에 있다	There are many apples on it.
10	tree	나무	She's planting a mango tree.

 Memo

 Memo

Answers

Student Book Answers

Lesson 1 At Home

A. Listen and number.   p. 8

| 4 | 1 | 5 |
| 3 | 6 | 2 |

Lesson 2 Family

A. Listen and circle.   p. 12

1. ⓐ   2. ⓑ   3. ⓑ   4. ⓐ

Lesson 3 This Is My Mom

B. Listen and number.   p. 14

| 1 | 4 | 2 | 3 |

C. Read and match.   p. 15

1. She is _____. •   • Bobo's brother
2. He is _____.   •   • Penny
3. This is _____. •   • Bobo's mom

Reading Time   p. 17

1. ⓐ   2. ⓑ

Lesson 4 Rooms

A. Listen and choose O or X.   p. 20

1. ○   2. ○   3. ○   4. ✕

Lesson 5 Furniture

A. Look and match.   p. 24

1. There is my closet.

2. There is my lamp.

3. There is my bookcase.

C. Connect, color, and say.   p. 25

Lesson 6 This Is the Kitchen

B. Listen and circle.   p. 26

1. ⓐ   2. ⓑ   3. ⓑ

C. Read and choose T or F.   p. 27

1. T   2. T

Reading Time   p. 29

1. ⓐ   2. ⓑ

Lesson 7 Possessions

A. Listen and number.   p. 32

| 3 | 1 | 4 |

| 2 | 6 | 5 |

Lesson 8 Numbers

A. Listen and circle.   p. 36

1. ⓐ   2. ⓑ   3. ⓑ   4. ⓑ

C. Find, color, and say.   p. 37

eggs	⊘⊘⊘⊘⊘⊘⊘⊘⊘⊘⊘⊘⊘⊘⊘⊘
cookies	🍪🍪🍪🍪🍪🍪🍪🍪🍪🍪🍪🍪🍪🍪🍪🍪
candies	🍬🍬🍬🍬🍬🍬🍬🍬🍬🍬🍬🍬🍬🍬🍬

Lesson 9 Do You Have Eggs?

B. Listen and choose O or X.   p. 38

1. O   2. ✕   3. ✕

C. Read and circle.   p. 39

1. ⓐ   2. ⓑ

Reading Time   p. 41

1. ⓐ   2. ⓐ

Lesson 10 Assessment Test 1

Listening   pp. 42~43

A. 1.   2.   3.

B. 1. O   2. ✕   3. ✕   4. O   5. O   6. ✕

C. 1.   2.   3.

4.   5.   6.

D.

② ③ ① ④

Reading   p. 44

Writing   p. 44

1.    This is my brother.

2. She's my sister.

3.   I have fourteen cows.

4. There is my lamp.

Speaking   p. 45

A. 1. Wow, it's nice.

2. It looks nice.

3. Nice to meet you, Chris.

4. He's my uncle.

5. Sure, I love them.

6. I have eleven puppies.

B. 1. He's my uncle.   2. Sure.

3. It looks nice.   4. I have fifteen pigs.

Lesson 11 Foods

A. Look and match.   p. 48

1. Would you like some noodles?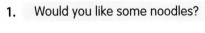

2. Would you like some steak?

3. Would you like some salad?

Lesson 12 Desserts

A. Listen and choose T or F.   p. 52

1. T   2. F   3. T   4. T

Lesson 13 It Smells Good

B. Listen and number.   p. 54

3   2   1   4

C. Read and circle.   p. 55

Reading Time   p. 57

1. ⓑ   2. ⓐ

Lesson 14 Outdoor Fun

A. Listen and number.   p. 60

6   2   4

5   1   3

C. Connect, color, and say.

Lesson 15 Describing Things

A. Look, match, and trace.   p. 64

1.   It's small and yellow.

2.   It's square and orange.

3.   It's long and yellow.

C. Ask, answer, and write.   p. 65

It's small.   It's long.   It's short.

Lesson 16 What a Nice Slide!

B. Listen and circle.   p. 66

1. ⓐ   2. ⓑ   3. ⓑ

C. Read and choose T or F.   p. 67

1. T   2. F

Reading Time   p. 69

1. ⓑ   2. ⓑ

Lesson 17 Things to Read

A. Listen and circle.   p. 72

1. ⓑ   2. ⓑ   3. ⓑ   4. ⓑ

Lesson 18 Fruit Trees

A. Listen and choose T or F.   p. 76

1. F   2. T   3. T   4. T

Lesson 19 What Are You Doing?

B. Listen and choose O or X.   p. 78

1. ✕   2. O   3. O

C. Read and match.
p. 79

1. Bobo came to _____.

2. Penny is reading _____.

3. The monkey is planting _____.

- a mango tree
- a magazine
- Penny's house

Reading Time
p. 81

1. ⓑ   2. ⓐ

Lesson 20 Assesment Test 2

Listening
pp. 82~83

A. 1.   2.   3.

B. 1. ○   2. ✕   3. ✕   4. ✕   5. ○   6. ○

C. 1.   2.   3.

4.   5.   6.

D.  ③   ②    ④   ①

Reading
p. 84

1.   2.   3.

4.   5.   6.

Writing
p. 84

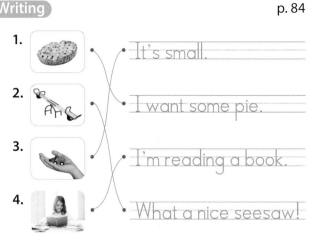

1. — It's small.
2. — I want some pie.
3. — I'm reading a book.
4. — What a nice seesaw!

Speaking
p. 85

A. 1. I think so, too.
2. Yes, I'm coming.
3. I'm reading a newspaper.
4. It's long and yellow.
5. Yes, please.
6. I want some pie.

B. 1. I want some ice cream.
2. That's a good idea.
3. It's small.
4. I'm reading a book.

Workbook
Answers

Lesson 1 At Home
pp. 4~5

A. 1. ⓐ Hi. Please come in.

ⓑ Thanks.

2. ⓐ Mom, this is Ben. Ben, this is my mom.

ⓑ Nice to meet you, Ben.

B. 1. Hi. Please come in.

2. Thanks.

C. 1. mom   This is my mom.

2. grandpa   This is my grandpa.

3. dad   This is my dad.

4. grandma   This is my grandma.

Lesson 2 Family
p. 6~7

A. 1. ⓐ Thank you.

ⓑ Have a seat.

2. ⓐ Who is she?

ⓑ She's my sister.

B.

1.   Thank you.

2.   Have a seat.

C.

Who is he?

1. He's my uncle.

3. He's my brother.

Who is she?

2. She's my aunt.

4. She's my sister.

Lesson 3 This Is My Mom

pp. 8~9

A. Thanks.

Who is he?

She's my mom.

Nice to meet you.

B. 1. ⓑ Who is she?

2. ⓑ This is my brother.

3. ⓐ He's my uncle.

4. ⓐ This is my mom.

C. 1. work

2. smile

3. sing

4. family

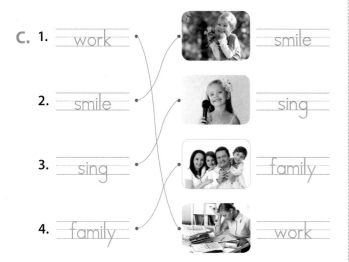

smile

sing

family

work

Lesson 4 Rooms

pp. 10~11

A. 1. ⓐ Come with me.

ⓑ Okay.

2. ⓐ This is the kitchen.

ⓑ Wow, it's nice.

B. 1. Have a seat.

2. Come with me.

3. Okay.

C. 1. This is the bathroom.

2. This is the bedroom.

3. This is the living room.

4. This is the kitchen.

 Wow, it's nice.

Lesson 5 Furniture

pp. 12~13

A. 1. ⓐ Sure.

ⓑ May I use your bathroom?

2. ⓐ This is my room. There is my bed.

ⓑ It looks nice.

B. **1.** ⓐ May I use your bathroom?

2. ⓑ Sure.

C.

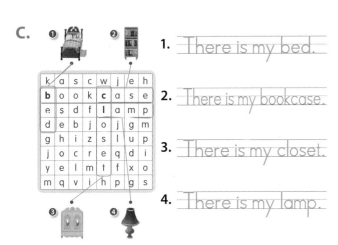

1. There is my bed.

2. There is my bookcase.

3. There is my closet.

4. There is my lamp.

Lesson 6 This Is the Kitchen
pp. 14~15

A. Come with me.

This is the kitchen.

May I use your bedroom?

There is my bed.

B. **1.** kitchen   This is the kitchen.

2. bedroom   This is the bedroom.

3. closet   There is my closet.

4. bed   There is my bed.

C.

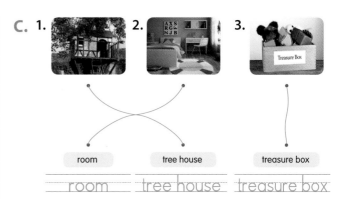

| room | tree house | treasure box |

room   tree house   treasure box

Lesson 7 Possessions
pp. 16~17

A. **1.** ⓐ Sure, I love them.

ⓑ Do you like puppies?

2. ⓐ Yes, I do.

ⓑ Do you have horses?

B. **1.** Do you like puppies?

2. Come with me.

3. Sure, I love them.

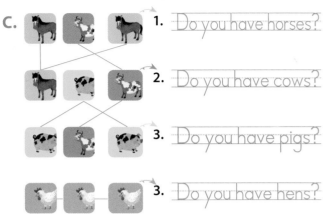

C.
1. Do you have horses?
2. Do you have cows?
3. Do you have pigs?
3. Do you have hens?

Lesson 8 Numbers

A. 1. ⓐ Can I touch them?
ⓑ Sure, you can.

2. ⓐ I have eleven eggs.
ⓑ How many eggs do you have?

B.
1.
Can I touch them?
⋮
Sure, you can.

2.
Do you like puppies?
⋮
Sure, I love them.

C. How many eggs do you have?
1. I have eleven eggs.
2. I have thirteen eggs.
3. I have fifteen eggs.
4. I have twelve eggs.
5. I have fourteen eggs.

Lesson 9 Do You Have Eggs?

A.
Sure, I love them.
Do you have eggs?
I have fifteen eggs.
Sure, you can.

B.
1. horses | Do you have horses?
2. cows | How many cows do you have?
3. fourteen | I have fourteen eggs.

C. 1. nest   2. egg
3. chick   4. hen

Lesson 11 Foods

A. 1. ⓐ It smells good.
ⓑ Yes, it does!

2. ⓐ Yes, please.

　　ⓑ Would you like some noodles?

B. 1. It smells good.　**2.** Can I touch them?

Sure, you can.　Yes, it does!

C. 1. noodles　Would you like some noodles?

2. salad　Would you like some salad?

3. soup　Would you like some soup?

4. steak　Would you like some steak?

Lesson 12 Desserts
pp. 24~25

A. 1. ⓐ Thank you.

　　ⓑ Help yourself.

2. ⓐ I want some pudding.

　　ⓑ What do you want for dessert?

B. 1. ⓑ Help yourself.

2. ⓐ Thank you.

C. What do you want for dessert?

1. I want some pudding.

2. I want some pie.

3. I want some crackers.

4. I want some ice cream.

Lesson 13 It Smells Good
pp. 26~27

A. It smells good.

Yes, it does!

Yes, please.

Help yourself.

B. 1. ➡ Would you like some noodles?

2. Would you like some steak?

➡ Would you like some salad?

3. I want some ice cream.

➡ I want some pie.

C. 1. refrigerator

2. blender

3. milk

4. banana smoothie

Lesson 14 Outdoor Fun   pp. 28~29

A. 1. ⓐ Let's go outside.

ⓑ That's a good idea.

2. ⓐ What a nice slide!

ⓑ I think so, too.

B. 1. Let's go outside.

2. That's a good idea.

C. ❶ slide ❷ seesaw

1. What a nice slide!

2. What a nice seesaw!

3. What a nice swing!

4. What a nice bench!

❸ swing ❹ bench

Lesson 15 Describing Things   pp. 30~31

A. 1. ⓐ Okay. I'm coming.

ⓑ Can you help me?

2. ⓐ What does it look like?

ⓑ It's big.

B. 1. Can you help me?   ○

2. Let's go outside.   ✕

3. Okay. I'm coming.   ○

C. What does it look like?

1. big   It's big.

2. long   It's long.

3. small   It's small.

4. short   It's short.

Lesson 16 What a Nice Slide!   pp. 32~33

A. ● What a nice slide!

   ● Can you help me?

   ● It's small and red.

   ● Thank you so much.

B. 1. ⓑ What a nice seesaw!

   2. ⓐ What a nice swing!

   3. ⓑ It's small.

   4. ⓐ It's long and yellow.

C. 1. Big Ben
   2. the Eiffel Tower
   3. the Statue of Liberty
   4. the Great Wall

   England
   the U.S.
   China
   France

2. ⓐ I'm reading a book.

   ⓑ What are you doing?

B. 1. I had fun.

   2. Me, too.

   3. I'm coming.

C.

   1. I'm reading a newspaper.

   2. I'm reading a letter.

   3. I'm reading a book.

   4. I'm reading a magazine.

Lesson 17 Things to Read   pp. 34~35

A. 1. ⓐ I had fun.

   ⓑ Me, too.

Lesson 18 Fruit Trees   pp. 36~37

A. 1. ⓐ Of course.

   ⓑ Can I come again?

2. ⓐ What is he doing?

ⓑ He's planting a lemon tree.

B. 1.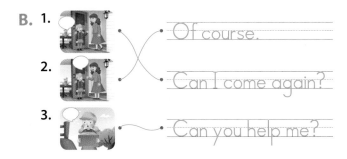

Of course.

2.

Can I come again?

3.

Can you help me?

C. 1. He's planting a pear tree.

2. He's planting a peach tree.

3. He's planting a lemon tree.

4. He's planting a mango tree.

Lesson 19 What Are You Doing? pp. 38~39

A. 🏆 What are you doing?

🌀 What is she doing?

🏆 I had fun.

☘ What a nice tree!

B. 1. letter   I'm reading a letter.

2. newspaper   I'm reading a newspaper.

3. peach tree   He's planting a peach tree.

4. pear tree   He's planting a pear tree.

C. 1. pick

2. best

3. yummy

4. apple jam

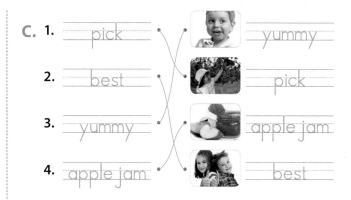

yummy

pick

apple jam

best

- - - - - - - - - - - - - - - - - - - -

Final Test
English Town Starter Book 3

1. ②	2. ②	3. ④	4. ⑤	5. ②
6. ①	7. ②	8. ①	9. ④	10. ③
11. ⑤	12. ④	13. ①	14. ①	15. ①
16. ②	17. ③	18. ④		
19. bathroom	20. big			

Memo

ENGLiSH TOWN

FOR EVERYONE

STARTER

BOOK 3

WORKBOOK

YBM

ENGLISH TOWN

FOR EVERYONE

STARTER

BOOK

3

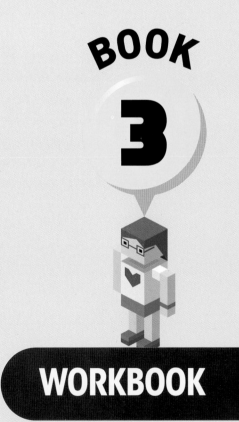

WORKBOOK

Contents

1. At Home

A. Trace and choose.

1
  ⓐ Hi. Please come in.

  ⓑ Thanks.

2
  ⓐ Mom, this is Ben. Ben, this is my mom.

  ⓑ Nice to meet you, Ben.

B. Follow the line and trace.

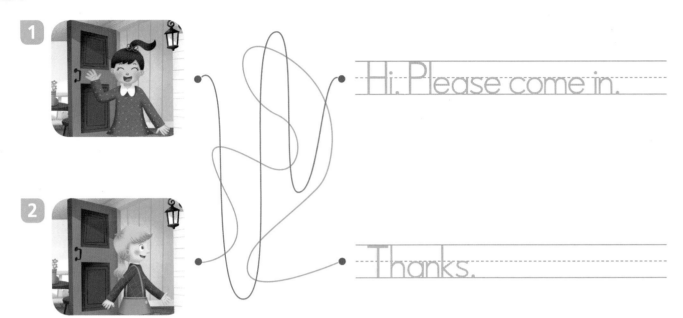

1 Hi. Please come in.

2 Thanks.

C. Check and write.

1 ☑ mom
   ☐ grandpa

This is my mom.

2 ☐ grandpa
   ☐ grandma

This is my

3 ☐ dad
   ☐ grandma

This is my

4 ☐ mom
   ☐ grandma

This is my

Lesson 2 Family

A. Trace and choose.

1

    ⓐ Thank you.

    ⓑ Have a seat.

2

    ⓐ Who is she?

    ⓑ She's my sister.

B. Match and trace.

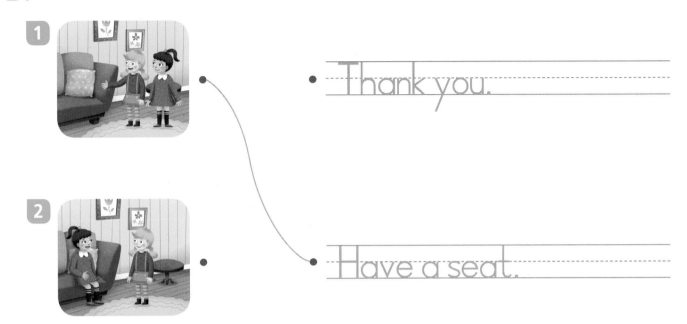

1

2

Thank you.

Have a seat.

C. Choose and write.

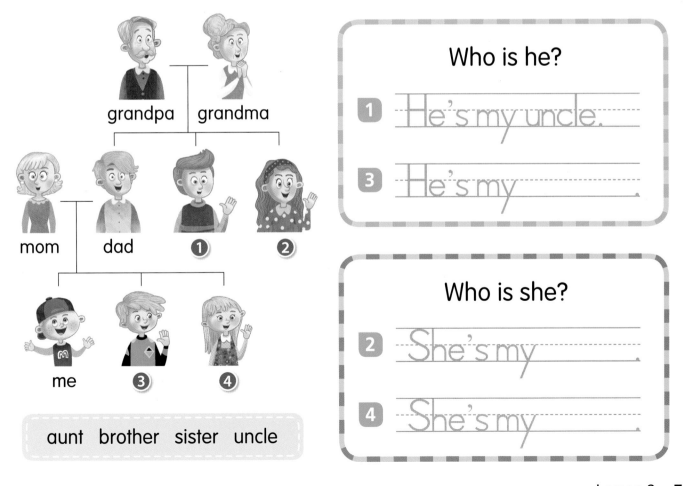

grandpa grandma

mom dad ❶ ❷

me ❸ ❹

aunt brother sister uncle

Who is he?

1 He's my uncle.

3 He's my _____.

Who is she?

2 She's my _____.

4 She's my _____.

This Is My Mom

A. Read and complete.

- She's my mom.
- Who is he?
- Thanks.
- Nice to meet you.

 Hi. Please come in.

 Thanks.

 _____

He's my brother.

 Who is she?

_____

 Mom, this is Penny.
Penny, this is my mom.

 _____

8

B. Circle and write.

 1

ⓐ Who is he?
ⓑ Who is she?

Who is she?

2

ⓐ This is my sister.
ⓑ This is my brother.

3

ⓐ He's my uncle.
ⓑ He's my grandpa.

4

ⓐ This is my mom.
ⓑ This is my dad.

C. Trace, match, and rewrite.

1

work •

•

2

smile •

•

3

sing •

•

4

family •

• work

Lesson 4 Rooms

A. Trace and choose.

1. ⓐ Come with me.

    ⓑ Okay.

2. ⓐ This is the kitchen.

    ⓑ Wow, it's nice.

B. Follow the line and trace.

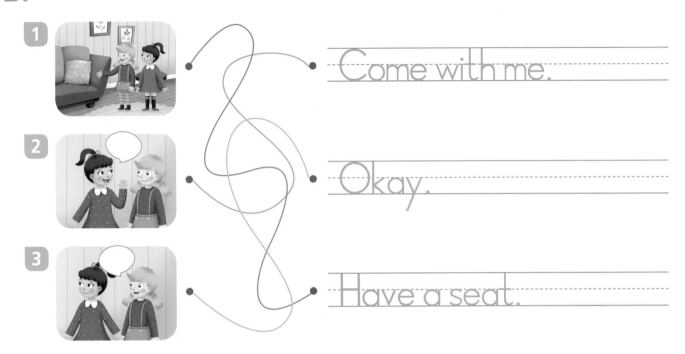

1 Come with me.

2 Okay.

3 Have a seat.

C. Choose and write.

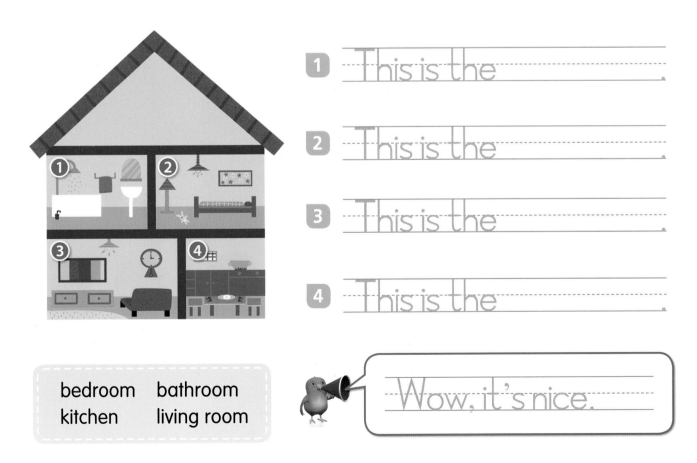

1 This is the _____.

2 This is the _____.

3 This is the _____.

4 This is the _____.

bedroom   bathroom
kitchen   living room

Wow, it's nice.

5 Furniture

A. Trace and choose.

1
a Sure.

b May I use your bathroom?

2
a This is my room. There is my bed.

b It looks nice.

B. Circle and trace.

(a) May I use your bathroom?

(b) May I use your bedroom?

(a) No, thank you.

(b) Sure.

C. Find, match, and write.

①  ②

k	a	s	c	w	j	e	h
b	o	o	k	c	a	s	e
e	s	d	f	l	a	m	p
d	e	b	j	o	j	g	m
g	h	i	z	s	l	u	p
j	o	c	r	e	q	d	i
y	e	l	m	t	f	x	o
m	q	v	i	h	p	g	s

③   ④

1 A: There is my bed.
  B: It looks nice.

2 A: There is my _____.
  B: It looks nice.

3 A: There is my _____.
  B: It looks nice.

4 A: There is my _____.
  B: It looks nice.

6 This Is the Kitchen

A. Read and complete.

- There is my bed.
- Come with me.
- May I use your bedroom?
- This is the kitchen.

 _____

 Okay.

 _____

Wow, it's nice.

 _____

Sure.

 _____

It looks nice.

14

B. Check and write.

1. ☐ kitchen
   ☐ bathroom

   This is the _____ .

2. ☐ bedroom
   ☐ living room

   This is the _____ .

3. ☐ lamp
   ☐ closet

   There is my _____ .

4. ☐ bed
   ☐ bookcase

   There is my _____ .

C. Match and write.

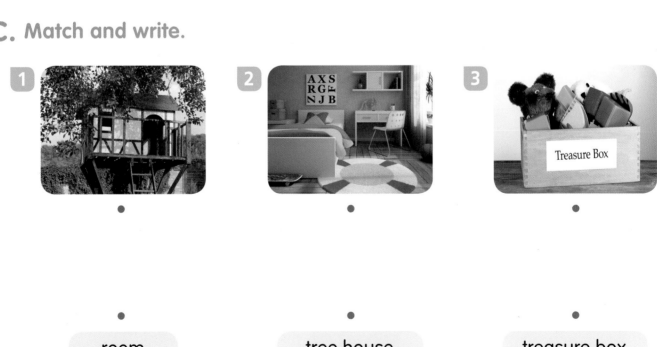

room

tree house

treasure box

room _____

_____

_____

Possessions

A. Trace and choose.

1
  a Sure, I love them.

  b Do you like puppies?

2
  a Yes, I do.

  b Do you have horses?

B. Follow the line and trace.

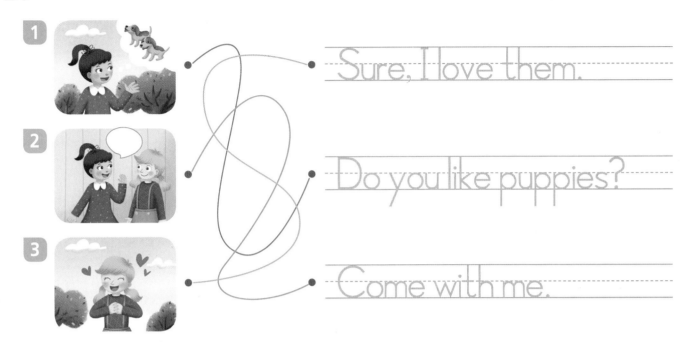

1. Sure, I love them.
2. Do you like puppies?
3. Come with me.

C. Connect and write.

cows   hens   horses   pigs

1. A: Do you have horses?
   B: Yes, I do.

2. A: Do you have _____?
   B: Yes, I do.

3. A: Do you have _____?
   B: Yes, I do.

4. A: Do you have _____?
   B: Yes, I do.

Lesson 8 Numbers

A. Trace and choose.

1
 ⓐ Can I touch them?

 ⓑ Sure, you can.

2
 ⓐ I have eleven eggs.

 ⓑ How many eggs do you have?

B. Match and trace.

1. Can I touch them?

•

•

Sure, you can.

2. Do you like puppies?

•

•

Sure, I love them.

C. Add and write.

| eleven | twelve | thirteen | fourteen | fifteen |

  How many eggs do you have?

1. $10 + 1 =$ I have eleven eggs.

2. $10 + 3 =$ I have _____ eggs.

3. $10 + 5 =$ I have _____ eggs.

4. $10 + 2 =$ I have _____ eggs.

5. $10 + 4 =$ I have _____ eggs.

9 Do You Have Eggs?

A. Read and complete.

> • Do you have eggs? • Sure, I love them.
> • Sure, you can. • I have fifteen eggs.

 Do you like chickens?

 _____

 _____

 Yes, I do.

 How many eggs do you have?

 _____

 Can I touch them?

 _____

B. Circle and write.

1
(horses)
pigs

Do you have _____ ?

2
hens
cows

How many _____ do you have?

3
fourteen
fifteen

I have _____ eggs.

C. Choose and write.

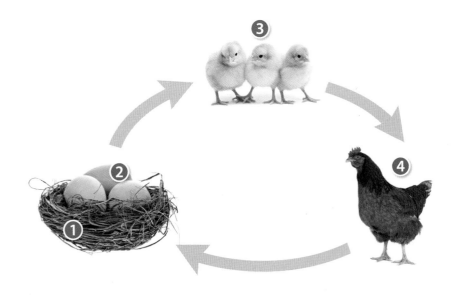

egg
hen
nest
chick

1 _____

2 _____

3 _____

4 _____

Foods

1 ⓐ It smells good.

ⓑ Yes, it does!

2 ⓐ Yes, please.

ⓑ Would you like some noodles?

B. Match and trace.

1 ‑‑‑‑It smells good.‑‑‑‑

2 ‑‑‑‑Can I touch them?‑‑‑‑

‑‑‑‑Sure, you can.‑‑‑‑

‑‑‑‑Yes, it does!‑‑‑‑

C. Circle and write.

1

steak
noodles

A: ‑‑‑‑Would you like some‑‑‑‑ ?

B: Yes, please.

2

salad
bread

A: ‑‑‑‑Would you like some‑‑‑‑ ?

B: Yes, please.

3

soup
salad

A: ‑‑‑‑Would you like some‑‑‑‑ ?

B: Yes, please.

4

fish
steak

A: ‑‑‑‑Would you like some‑‑‑‑ ?

B: Yes, please.

12 Desserts

A. Trace and choose.

1
 ⓐ Thank you.

 ⓑ Help yourself.

2
 ⓐ I want some pudding.

 ⓑ What do you want for dessert?

B. Circle and trace.

1

    a Have a seat.

    b Help yourself.

2

    a Thank you.

    b It looks nice.

C. Choose and write.

crackers   ice cream   pie   pudding

What do you want for dessert?

1 I want some

2 I want some

3 I want some

4 I want some

13 It Smells Good

A. Read and complete.

- Yes, please.
- It smells good.
- Yes, it does!
- Help yourself.

_____

_____

Would you like some noodles?

_____

_____

Thank you.

What do you want for dessert?

I want some pudding, pie, crackers, and ice cream.

26

B. Find a mistake and correct.

| noodles | ice cream | pie | salad | steak | pudding |

1 Would you like some ~~crackers~~?

➡ Would you like some _____?

2 Would you like some steak?

➡ _____

3 I want some ice cream.

➡ _____

C. Choose and write.

| banana smoothie | blender | milk | refrigerator |

1

_____

2

_____

3

_____

4

_____

14 Outdoor Fun

A. Trace and choose.

1. **a** Let's go outside.
   b That's a good idea.

2. **a** What a nice slide!
   b I think so, too.

B. Trace and match.

1

Let's go outside. •

2

That's a good idea. •

C. Match and write.

❶ slide   **❷** seesaw

•   •

•   •

•   •

❸ swing   **❹** bench

1 A: What a nice _____ !

B: I think so, too.

2 A: What a nice _____ !

B: I think so, too.

3 A: What a nice _____ !

B: I think so, too.

4 A: What a nice _____ !

B: I think so, too.

Describing Things

A. Trace and choose.

1
  ⓐ Okay. I'm coming.

  ⓑ Can you help me?

2
  ⓐ What does it look like?

  ⓑ It's big.

B. Trace and choose O or X.

1. Can you help me? Ⓞ X

2. Let's go outside. O X

3. Okay. I'm coming. O X

C. Circle and write.

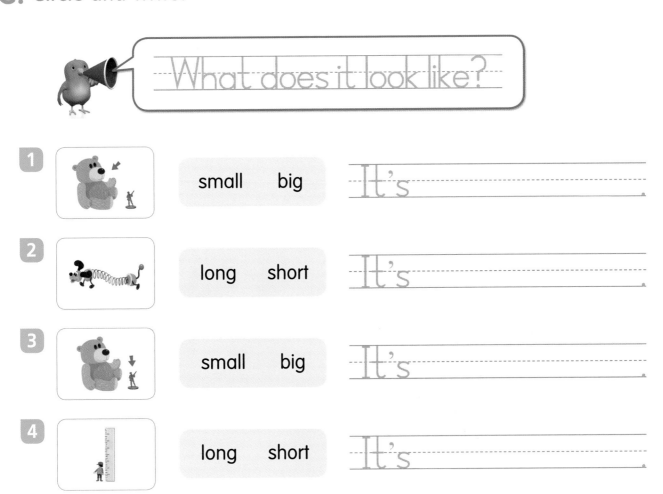

What does it look like?

1. small   big   It's _____

2. long   short   It's _____

3. small   big   It's _____

4. long   short   It's _____

16 What a Nice Slide!

A. Read and complete.

- Can you help me?
- What a nice slide!
- It's small and red.
- Thank you so much.

 _____

 I think so, too.

 _____

Okay. I'm coming.

What does it look like?

_____

_____

 You're welcome.

B. Circle and write.

1

  a What a nice slide!

  b What a nice seesaw!

2

  a What a nice swing!

  b What a nice bench!

3

  a It's big.

  b It's small.

4

  a It's long and yellow.

  b It's short and yellow.

C. Trace and match.

1 Big Ben      England

2 the Eiffel Tower      the U.S.

3 the Statue of Liberty      China

4 the Great Wall      France

Things to Read

A. Trace and choose.

1. a I had fun.

   b Me, too.

2. a I'm reading a book.

   b What are you doing?

B. Follow the line and trace.

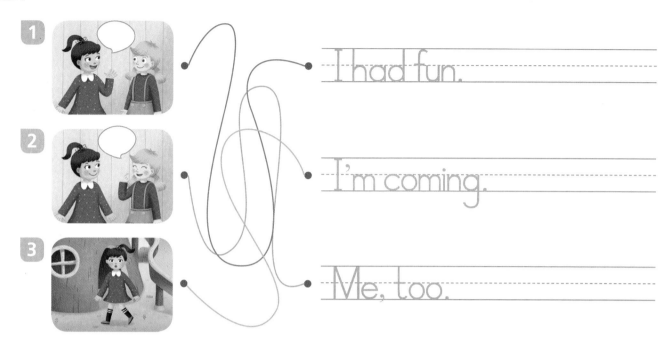

I had fun.

I'm coming.

Me, too.

C. Find, match, and write.

letter   newspaper   book   magazine

c	l	f	i	e	m	o	d	b
n	e	w	s	p	a	p	e	r
a	t	g	l	m	g	b	m	u
b	t	h	k	q	a	g	h	w
n	e	p	s	e	z	c	u	v
d	r	i	b	e	i	f	k	y
c	g	o	x	p	n	g	j	l
b	o	o	k	h	e	m	b	e

1 I'm reading a

2 I'm reading a

3 I'm reading a

4 I'm reading a

18 Fruit Trees

A. Trace and choose.

1
  ⓐ Of course.

  ⓑ Can I come again?

2
  ⓐ What is he doing?

  ⓑ He's planting a lemon tree.

B. Match and trace.

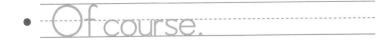

Of course.

Can I come again?

Can you help me?

C. Choose and write.

lemon   mango   peach   pear

1. A: What is he doing?

B: He's planting a   tree.

2. A: What is he doing?

B: He's planting a   tree.

3. A: What is he doing?

B: He's planting a   tree.

4. A: What is he doing?

B: He's planting a   tree.

19 What Are You Doing?

A. Read and complete.

- I had fun.
- What a nice tree!
- What is she doing?
- What are you doing?

 _____

_____

 I'm reading a magazine.

She's planting a mango tree.

_____

 Me, too.

_____

38

B. Circle and write.

1. letter
   book

   I'm reading a _____.

2. magazine
   newspaper

   I'm reading a _____.

3. peach tree
   mango tree

   He's planting a _____.

4. lemon tree
   pear tree

   He's planting a _____.

C. Trace, match, and rewrite.

1. pick •

2. best •

3. yummy •

4. apple jam •

Memo